Humpty Who?

A Crash Course in 80 Nursery Rhymes for Clueless Moms and Dads

Includes a CD with 35 Songs

by Jennifer Griffin

WORKMAN PUBLISHING · NEW YORK

For Luke

Library of Congress Cataloging-in-Publication Data is available.
ISBN-13: 978-0-7611-4368-0

Workman books are available at special discounts when purchased in bulk for premiums and sales promotions as well as for fund-raising or educational use. Special editions or book excerpts can be created to specification. For details, contact the Special Sales Director at the address below.

Workman Publishing Company, Inc.
225 Varick Street
New York, NY 10014-4381
www.workman.com

Printed in China
First printing August 2007
10 9 8 7 6 5 4 3 2

CD produced & arranged by Jamie Lawrence. Recorded by Daniel Lawrence. Assisted by Samuel Giannelli and Dan Hopler. 2nd Assistant: Adam Broza. Mixed and mastered by Jamie Lawrence. Recorded, mixed, and mastered at Manhattan Beach Recording, NYC, April/May 2007. All public domain arrangements © 2007 Elliot Music Co. Inc. ASCAP. No animals were harmed in the making of this CD. All animal sounds were performed by the cast.

Contents

- - - - - - -

Acknowledgments

- - - - - - - - - - -

"What do you say . . .?" Thank you!

Thanks to all the people who helped bring *Humpty Who?* to life.

At Workman, Suzie Bolotin, David Allender, and Paul Hanson championed the book early in its life. Peter Workman decided to publish it. Ruth Sullivan is as amazing an editor as I had always heard, and I am grateful to have worked with her. I am thankful to her assistant, Maisie Tivnan, as well. Paul Gamarello and Barbara Balch have ensured that the book looks its best.

Many friends and colleagues shared advice and favorite nursery rhymes with me, including Nanni Froelich; Sharon Bowers; Vidia Bridgemohan; Lisa Kuklinski-Ramirez and Jorge Ramirez; members of the Desmaison family, especially Roselyne; members of the Griffin family, especially Wynne and Carol; Samantha Bruce-Benjamin and her mother; Anne Cherry; and parents and teachers of the 43rd Street Kids Preschool, especially Lynne Phillips and Carolyn Montgomery.

The CD accompanying this book is the result of work by Jamie Lawrence, Rebecca Kendall, Carolyn Montgomery, and Margaret Murphy. I am delighted by and very grateful for their efforts.

Finally, thanks to Christophe for his help in the creation of this project and in the creation of Luke, who inspired it.

Humpty Who?

If You're Clueless and You Know It, Clap Your Hands

Parenthood is a time of joy and wonder. The first giggle and coo, the first step, the first word. It's all miraculous. But for many first-time parents babyhood is also a time of bafflement and anxiety. In many ways we know what to expect, but no matter how prepared we are, we will still have questions. There is no way ever to be fully prepared. For me, it was the baby shower that underscored how little I knew. What is A&D and why do I need a gallon of it? What circumstances call for a cotton ball? This onesie is lovely, thank you. Is it sleepwear or something the child can wear to a restaurant?

My son arrived and many of my questions seemed to answer themselves. (A&D is used to prevent diaper rash, cotton balls are for battling cradle cap, and onesies are for sleeping and dining out, FYI.) I was well prepared, after all. And the few issues that did arise—dealing with teething, sleeping strategies, breast-feeding advice, handling a fever—were ably covered in my parenting books. It was smooth sailing—until one fateful day.

It was a few weeks into my son's life. The relatives had gone home, visits from friends were slowing down, my husband was back at work. Suddenly it was just me and the baby with long days stretching out before us. And on this particular day, my bundle of joy was cranky. Very cranky.

I fed him. I changed him.

I tried to get him to nap. I gave him a binkie. I took him for a stroll. I rocked him. I repeated the sequence, but with no results. Finally, I groped for something to sing to him. Anything would do. It would just have to be catchy and upbeat. Anything at all. Forgive me. I was very tired. I was astonished to hear these words escape my lips:

"Confident, confident, dry and secure. Raise your hands, raise your hands if you're sure."

Was that the best I could do? I tried again.

"Love, exciting and new. Come aboard, we're expecting you."

The theme song from an Aaron Spelling TV show? I racked my brains for more material and took another shot.

"Dashing through the snow"—did I

mention it was spring?—*"In a one-horse open sleigh. . . ."* But my son seemed satisfied and I knew all the words, *"O'er the fields we go"*—it was unseasonal, but otherwise it was working out—*"Laughing all the way. Ha Ha Ha."*

Eventually my son settled down and went back to sleep, giving me time to reflect. How could this have happened? Did I really not know any nursery rhymes, songs, lullabies—*anything* that was appropriate for an infant? I took inventory and came up with a few fragments, some first lines, but little else. I knew that the wheels on the bus went round and round, but I didn't know what the other parts of the bus did. I knew that little stars twinkled, but I couldn't tell you more about them than that. And every time I recited "The Queen of Hearts," Miss

Muffet somehow appeared at the end. Was I missing a gene? Was there a hormonal imbalance blocking my memory of these universally known ditties? Or had I just never learned them in the first place?

I had planned to keep this seismic gap in my knowledge a secret. Nobody needed to know that I didn't know what a tuffet was. It was nothing a little cramming couldn't fix. But a funny thing happened on the road to nursery verse literacy: I realized I was not alone. Many mothers of my acquaintance, I learned as I tentatively owned up to the gaps in my knowledge, were Mother Goose-challenged. Somehow we'd thought of everything else, but we hadn't brushed up on the nursery verses that have soothed and entertained generations of children.

This book seeks to remedy that. It contains my eighty favorite classic nursery rhymes along with instructions on how to perform them and a bit of history on their origins. My hope is that the book will give you and your baby pleasure, comfort, and confidence. When you learn the origins of "Pease Porridge Hot" (page 112), you'll feel better if you, like me, have ever sung your child a commercial jingle. And when you understand more about the bawdy origins of Rub-a-Dub-Dub (page 132), you'll realize that almost anything is okay to sing to a child, as long as it's catchy. I hope that my thoughts on emoting (page 118) free you to be goofy, because babies love broad humor and most of all they love you—no matter how silly or off-key you are. You are Madonna, as far as they are concerned.

Maybe you'll pick up a few tips as well, such as the miracle of the yoga *om* and its applications (page 179). And if you master even a quarter of the classics here, I guarantee years' worth of coos and giggles and snuggles and repetitions of that magic word that proves you really have done your job well: "Again!"

Useful Tips for Enjoying this Book with Your Child

On the History of Nursery Verse

Nursery rhymes have been around as long as children have. Mothers from time immemorial have soothed and amused their little ones with words and song. A few of those words and songs have become so popular that they were passed down over generations. Most nursery rhymes that we've come to think of as classic originated in England and are hundreds of years old. These include "Humpty Dumpty," "Hey Diddle Diddle," "Little Boy Blue," and "The Noble Duke of York," to name just a few.

Others have even older origins —"As I Was Going to St. Ives" is believed to be a variation of a riddle found in ancient Egypt. Some are American—"Mary Had a Little Lamb," for example, was written in New England in the nineteenth century. Other standards have caught on quickly: the last several decades have given us "Alice the Camel," "If All the Raindrops Were Lemon Drops and Gumdrops," and "The Wheels on the Bus."

I have included some foreign verses that have become popular in America or are so excellent, they should be, like the French lullaby "Fais Dodo" and a Spanish song about chickens, "Pío, Pío, Pío," as well as the multi-culti hit "Frère Jacques," which exists in nearly every language. Most of the verses, new and old, are by authors whose identities have been lost over time. In other surprising cases, the author is known: "Twinkle, Twinkle, Little Star" is a poem by an English woman named Jane Taylor, and "Wee Willie Winkie" was written by Scotsman William Miller.

Meet the Opies

Although some nursery rhymes and songs were written down and published, most were part of an oral tradition, passed down from mother to child across the generations. Many of these rhymes were recorded by enterprising authors along the way, who included them in collections of verses; others were lost. The couple we have to thank for making sure that most classic nursery rhymes were documented are the Opies. Peter and Iona Opie were scholars of folklore who became experts in the literature and games of childhood. They wrote scores of books, including their groundbreaking *The Lore and Language of Schoolchildren* and comprehensive reference works like *The Oxford Dictionary of Nursery Rhymes*, as well as several popular spin-offs. Peter Opie died in 1982. After his death Mrs. Opie donated the couple's vast collection of early and rare children's literature— some 20,000 volumes—to Oxford's Bodleian Library.

It may be the Opies we have to thank for the fact that nursery rhymes have become a sort of lingua franca of childhood. You can go to a playground anywhere in America and start singing

"Ring Around the Rosie" and be assured that most of the other parents and kids will know it too. There is something beautiful about little preliterate munchkins being able to communicate with one another in this universal language.

My Book, My Choices

Although the Opies are great experts on the subject of nursery rhymes, and although many other enthusiasts have appeared in the wake of their success, they are not the final word on what's right. You are. Since most nursery rhymes have been passed down through the generations orally, there are many variations in the words. Oral tradition recognizes no "correct version." I first met "The Brave Old Duke of York" as "The Noble Duke of York" and have used my version here because it sounds right to my ear. "Noble" sounds to me, well, noble. Either one would be equally entertaining to your pumpkin. There are loads of verses for "Pop Goes the Weasel" and nobody really knows in which order they should go, so I've made up an order I like. The French lullaby "Fais Dodo" traditionally starts "Fais dodo, Colas mon petit frère. . . ." Colas is probably an abbreviation of the name Nicolas, but it sounds strange to English-speaking ears and it interferes with the rhyme scheme, so I've dropped it. In places I've included lesser-known verses of rhymes I love; in others I've dropped those that seem stilted to me. I've been loose with some translations for the sake of meter and rhyme—"Wee Willie Winkie," which I translated from the Scots, is an example. My goal has been to balance entertainment value with good old-fashioned tradition.

Music and Lyrics

A big part of the entertainment value of many verses in this book is the music they are accompanied by. Some tunes like "ABC," "Mary Had a Little Lamb," and "Three Blind Mice" we already know off the top of our head. Others are unfamiliar. Most readers need introductions or refreshers to songs like "Les Petites Marionettes" and "Oh Mr. Sun." All the songs are easy to learn, easy to sing, and pleasing to young ears, hence their staying power. You'll note that several nursery rhyme tunes are recycled. "Frère Jacques" and "Where Is Thumbkin?" use the same music. Two other classic verses are sung to the same music as "ABC." Can you name them? (See page 14 for the answer.)

Which came first, the music or the lyrics? There is a bit of chicken-and-egg with nursery rhymes, since they've come down to us through oral tradition. In most cases, the music seems to have followed. "Twinkle, Twinkle, Little Star" and "Mary Had a Little Lamb," for example, were both published poems before they were assigned tunes. The only sure example of the music coming before the words in this collection is Brahms's "Lullaby and Good Night."

The CD included with this book, featuring the vocal talents of Rebecca Kendall, Carolyn Montgomery, and Margaret Murphy, and the arrangements of Jamie Lawrence, allows you to learn the tunes to unfamiliar songs and jog your memory anytime you have a lapse (see page 186). We have tried to arrange them so that you can also sit down with your baby or toddler and listen to the whole thing straight through.

On Proper Technique

Proper technique? Relax, I'm teasing you! There is no proper technique. There is no *right* way to perform "Itsy Bitsy Spider" or "The Noble Duke of York." You are not going to be graded on this, and believe me, your audience is quite accepting. Anything you dream up is right. So please don't worry about being perfect. That said, certain tricks will make things easier for you. If you remember to start "Itsy Bitsy" with your thumb touching your index finger, the spider will climb up the web more gracefully. When you master the art of the trot, you'll be able to use it not only for "The Noble Duke of York" but also "Trot, Trot to Boston" and "To Market, to Market to Buy a Fat Pig." And if you get a big reaction on something—my son is crazy about the way I create puppets for him in "Les Petites Marionettes"—you'll want to be able to replicate it reliably. Consistency makes that easier.

But if your spider gambols awkwardly and your trots are not textbook, so what?

The Show Must Go On

Many famous performers have suffered from stage fright: Laurence Olivier, Maria Callas, and Barbra Streisand leap to mind. Are you shy as well? Do you feel embarrassed getting up

in front of another person and performing? Time to get over it. Babies and toddlers love a ham. They like enthusiasm and broad movements, funny voices, dancing, improvisation. This is your chance to shine—the one time, maybe in your life, when you don't have to worry that your audience won't think you are the best performer in the world. I urge you to relax and go for it. Use your Ethel Merman voice to belt out "ABC." Sing "Pío, Pío, Pío" in the style of an opera singer. Enlist your spouse to sing all the rounds with you. There will be laughing, there will be singing along (or some semblance of it), there will be applause. (There might be crying, too, but that's unlikely to be related to your performance.)

There are so many things to feel awkward and nervous about after you've had a baby. Nursery rhymes shouldn't be one of them. Singing and playing and dancing with your little one should be filled with joy and disco moves and high notes you can't really hit and big finishes. There should be nothing holding you back. Your baby is only a baby once and, believe me, that time goes fast. So let it all hang out.

A Few Little Ditties for You and the Kiddies:
The Rhymes, Verses, and Songs

ABC (The Alphabet Song)

is simple, yes, but that doesn't mean it's not wonderful. And forgive me for insulting your intelligence by including the words here, but I think of the alphabet song as the little black dress of nursery verse. It's fun (memorable happy tune) and functional (baby is learning as you sing); a classic that never goes out of style.

Sound Familiar? Does the tune ring a bell? The music is the same as that for "Twinkle, Twinkle, Little Star" (page 173) and "Baa, Baa, Black Sheep" (page 26).

Alphabet Song

A - B - C - D - E - F - G

H - I - J - K - L - M - N - O - P

Q - R - S - T - U and V

W - X - Y and Z

Now I know my ABCs

Next time won't you sing with me?

Alice the Camel is a simple,

memorable song that takes your little one on a wiggly-jiggly lap ride. Not part of the Old Mother Goose tradition, it's a contemporary number that has quickly become classic. (Listen to the CD if you don't know the tune.) Camels are fascinating to children for their mysterious water-carrying humps—you'll start seeing them soon in children's books and at the zoo. The verse, in addition to featuring an exotic creature, may be baby's first countdown.

The Action Bounce your child on your knee throughout the song, and when a number is mentioned, hold up that many fingers to the child. At the last verse, make a zero sign and whinny/neigh if you feel like it.

ALICE THE CAMEL

Alice the camel has five humps.
Alice the camel has five humps.
Alice the camel has five humps.
So go, Alice, go!
Boom, boom, boom

Alice the camel has four humps.
Alice the camel has four humps.
Alice the camel has four humps.
So go, Alice, go!
Boom, boom, boom

Alice the camel has three humps.
Alice the camel has three humps.
Alice the camel has three humps.
So go, Alice, go!
Boom, boom, boom

There's more 👉

Alice the camel has two humps.
Alice the camel has two humps.
Alice the camel has two humps.
So go, Alice, go!
Boom, boom, boom

Alice the camel has one hump.
Alice the camel has one hump.
Alice the camel has one hump.
So go, Alice, go!
Boom, boom, boom

Alice the camel has no hump.
Alice the camel has no hump.
Alice the camel has no hump.
So Alice is a horse.

LE MOT JUSTE

The *Oxford English Dictionary* contains full entries for more than 170,000 words in use in English today. This gives us lots of options for expressing ourselves. Are you limiting yourself? Try replacing some of your usual vocabulary with words that are more fun; you might be amazed at the difference. Here is an experiment: Wet a sponge and wring it out over the tub or sink with your toddler. First say "wring, wring, wring," then try "squeeze, squeeze, squeeze" instead. *Squeeze* will get a giggle—it's simply a wackier word. Look for the most colorful, euphonious way to say things.

Alouette is believed to have originated in French Canada. It's a song about a lark who is being plucked before being cooked. You can sing it in French and learn a few new vocabulary words starting with *tête* (head) and *nez* (nose) or sing it in the English translation. The song takes brilliantly to variations, adding as many or as few body parts as you like. Don't miss the opportunity to mime the action of plucking upon your own little pheasant. Kids love to be plucked.

Sing On! A second verse goes like this:

Alouette, gentille alouette,
Alouette, je te plumerai.
Je te plumerai le nez
Je te plumerai le nez
Et le nez, et le nez
Et la tête, et la tête
Alouette.

For additional verses, use any one-syllable body part, such as:

Les joues: cheeks
Les yeux: eyes
Le cou: neck
Les ailes: wings
Le dos: back
Les pattes: feet
La queue: tail

ALOUETTE

Alouette, gentille alouette,
> Little pheasant, tasty little pheasant,

Alouette, je te plumerai
> Little pheasant, I will pluck you

Je te plumerai la tête,
> I will pluck you on your head,

Je te plumerai la tête,
> I will pluck you on your head,

Et la tête, et la tête
> Pluck your head, pluck your head

Alouette.
> Little pheasant.

As I Was Going to St. Ives

is a jaunty rhyme, a juicy riddle, and a kid's first trick question all rolled into one. It's a puzzler that may lay the foundation for a life of crossword puzzle, Scrabble, or Sudoku dominance. The rhyme is believed to have ancient origins. A piece of papyrus with a similar riddle involving cats was found in Egypt and dates to around 1700 B.C.E.

Guess! So just how many *were* going to St. Ives? Only one: the "I" of the verse. FYI, if everyone mentioned— and every thing, the sacks included— was going too, then the final tally would be a whopping 2,802.

⚘ AS I WAS GOING TO ST. IVES

As I was going to St. Ives,
I met a man with seven wives,
Each wife had seven sacks,
Each sack had seven cats,
Each cat had seven kits:
Kits, cats, sacks, wives,
How many were going to St. Ives?

A Tisket, A Tasket

What's a tisket? a tasket?! Calm down. These are nonsense words. Don't get your knickers in a twist over every mysterious little tisket, tuffet, or knick-knack paddy whack.

Jazz it Up Go to the record store and find the classic Ella Fitzgerald recording of this old favorite. Singing along with Ella is a very cool way to spend quality nursery time.

A Tisket, A Tasket

A tisket, a tasket
A green and yellow basket
I wrote a letter to my love
And on the way I dropped it.

I dropped it, I dropped it
And on the way I dropped it
A little boy, he picked it up
And put it in his pocket.

Baa, Baa, Black Sheep may

be baby's first protest song. Dating to the mid-eighteenth century, "Baa, Baa, Black Sheep" is a complaint about taxes. In the wool trade, which was the basis of England's wealth, the first bag of wool goes to the government (the master); the second to the lord of the land (or his wife—the dame); the third to the shepherd.

But "Baa, Baa, Black Sheep" can also serve as a reminder of the visit to the petting zoo and an opportunity to count to three. Count off the bags of wool with your fingers if you like, and feel free to replace "boy" with "girl."

Dark Secret Black sheep yield wool that is so dark it cannot be dyed. It was worth less money to shepherds, which is how the term "black sheep" came to mean a disappointment.

Baa, Baa, Black Sheep

Baa, baa, black sheep
Have you any wool?
Yes, sir, yes, sir
Three bags full.
One for my master
One for my dame
And one for the little boy
Who lives down the lane.
Baa, baa, black sheep
Have you any wool?
Yes, sir, yes, sir
Three bags full.

Banbury Cross can be recited when your child is on a rocking horse—a "cockhorse" is another name for a rocking horse—but of course it works just as well when she's on your lap. You can rock or trot to Banbury Cross. If another adult is in the room, have him make a clopping effect as you recite the poem for a nifty duet.

See the Cross Banbury is a town in Oxfordshire, England, that once boasted three prominent crosses, which evidently loomed large in the town's psyche. They were destroyed in the early 1600s, some 150 years before this verse appeared. A new cross was erected in 1859 and you can see it (along with a lot of traffic) live on www.banbury-cross.co.uk/webcam.htm

Banbury Cross

Ride a cockhorse to
    Banbury Cross
To see a fine lady upon
    a white horse
Rings on her fingers
    and bells on her toes
She shall have music
    wherever she goes.

Clean Up, Clean Up might seem like a prissy, forgettable little thing, but try singing it when it's time to pick up toys and you'll see it's a miracle. It is to tidying rooms what Pavlov's bell is to his dog's dinner. Maybe it's the whistle-while-you-work effect or the idea that doing something pleasurable while you do something disagreeable makes the unpleasant thing tolerable. All I know is that it works.

Clean up, clean up,
Everybody everywhere,
Clean up, clean up,
Everybody do your share.

Make it Personal! Insert your child's name into the last line if you like: "Come on Luke, you do your share." For two-syllable names, cut the "you": "Come on Lily, do your share," and so on.

DR. PAVLOV, I PRESUME?

Ivan Pavlov was a Russian psychologist famous for his experiments with dogs. He discovered that if you ring a bell every time you feed a dog, and then you ring a bell and don't actually bring food, the dog's body will react as though the food is forthcoming. This became known as conditioning.

Conditioning can be a mom's best friend. I have found that if you pair a verse (or song) with an activity, the verse acts as a trigger that spurs the activity. For instance, if you sing the "clean up" song (opposite) every time you clean up, your child will come to so closely associate the song with the activity that he will not resist it as he might if you just asked him to help. Ditto with lullabies. Certain lullabies make my son sleepy, not just because they are soporifics on their own, but because I have paired them with nap- and bedtime. One song I sing to him is an old French pop standard "Plus Je T'Embrasse." I wonder what will happen years from now if he's in a bar in Paris and the little trio in the corner strikes up this song. Will he fall asleep in his drink? One more thing to worry about. Stick to the classic lullabies, friends, and be very careful about powerful psychological tricks.

Do Your Ears Hang Low?

is a really silly song. How can ears hang that low? How can they wobble to and fro? Impossible, right? Not necessarily. Earlobes come in two varieties: attached and unattached. Most people have unattached earlobes because the gene for that is dominant, while attached earlobes are a recessive trait. Other recessive traits you can talk about with a toddler include straight hairlines (vs. widow's peaks), hitchhiker's thumbs, and the ability to roll your tongue. So most of us do have ears that hang low—but not that low. Who does have ears that hang low? Dogs! The next time you see a friendly dog with floppy ears—a basset hound, say—it's the perfect time to sing this song and play with ears.

♩ Do Your Ears Hang Low?

Do your ears hang low?
> *Press your wrists against your ears with your hands dangling down from them*

Do they wobble to and fro?
> *Swing your hands from side to side*

Can you tie them in a knot?
> *Mime tying a knot*

Can you tie them in a bow?
> *Mime tying a bow*

Can you throw them over your shoulder
> *Throw your hands over your shoulder*

Like a continental soldier?
> *Walk stiffly like a toy soldier; salute*

Do your ears hang low?
> *Press your wrists against your ears again, as at beginning*

Down by the Station

is a fun way to celebrate little kids' fascination with trains. It's a lovely round, so if you can get more than one person to sing, so much the better. The last two lines are not part of the song; they are just the sound of the trains chugging out of the station. Follow it up with "I've Been Working on the Railroad" if you like.

All Aboard! Pull the handle above you when the stationmaster does so. To mimic the motion of the big wheels in the last line: face your palms toward each other, shoulder-width apart, and move them in big circles as you make *choo-choo* noises.

DOWN BY THE STATION

Down by the station,
  early in the morning,
See the little puffer bellies
  all in a row.
Hear the station master
  pull upon the handle,
Puff puff, toot toot, off we go.
Choo-choo, choo-choo,
  choo-choo, choo-choo...

Fais Dodo is a classic French lullaby that's both easy to learn and very soothing—whether or not you speak French. (The music is included on the CD.) You'll notice a lot of "O" sounds in the verse. These sustained O's have some of the same soothing effects as the yoga *om* (page 179).

The Big Sleep *Dodo* is a French nickname for sleep. If you've returned to work after having a baby you might relate to an expression the French use when all they're doing is dragging themselves to work and then home to sleep: "métro, boulot, dodo," which translates as "subway, job, sleep." Remember when life was more like métro, boulot, bistro, disco, dodo? Me, too. Vaguely.

1º FAIS DODO

Fais dodo,   Go to sleep,

Mon petit frère   My little brother

Fais dodo,   Go to sleep,

T'auras du lolo.   You've had your milk.

Maman est en haut   Mother is upstairs

Qui fait du gâteau.   Making a cake.

Papa est en bas   Daddy is downstairs

Qui fait du chocolat.   Making hot chocolate.

Fais dodo,   Go to sleep,

Mon petit frère   My little brother

Fais dodo,   Go to sleep,

T'auras du lolo.   You've had your milk.

Frère Jacques is one of the nursery

all-stars. Classics are great, but they run the risk of becoming boring. One way to keep this sweet round fresh is to learn it in several languages. The song is a round, so the more the merrier. (The second group of singers can start at any point, but I think it sounds best at the second line.)

Parlez Vous . . . ?

Versions exist in German, Italian, Spanish, Polish, Dutch, and many other European languages. I offer a few here to keep you on your toes.

German

Bruder Jakob,
   Bruder Jakob,
Schlafst du noch?
   Schlafst du noch?
Hörst du nicht
   die Glocken,
Hörst du nicht
   die Glocken,
Ding, dang, dong.
   Ding, dang, dong.

Italian

Fra' Martino,
   campanaro,
Dormi tu?
   Dormi tu?
Suona le campane,
   suona le campane,
Din, don, dan.
   Din, don, dan.

Spanish

Fray Felipe,
   Fray Felipe,
¿Duermes tú?
   ¿Duermes tú?
Suenan las campanas,
   suenan las campanas,
Tan, Tan, Tan.
   Tan, Tan, Tan.

FRÈRE JACQUES

Frère Jacques, Frère Jacques,
Brother John, Brother John,

Dormez-vous? Dormez-vous?
Are you sleeping, are you sleeping?

Sonnez les matines, sonnez les matines,
Morning bells are ringing,
Morning bells are ringing,

Ding, dang, dong. Ding, dang, dong.
Ding, dang, dong. Ding, dang, dong.

Georgie Porgie is a perfect little rhyme to clap hands to and gives moms an opportunity to kiss adorable chubby cheeks (as if we needed one!). The only people I might hesitate to recite it to are little boys named George. Let's face it; no one wants to be associated with wimpy Georgie Porgie. Better to chuckle at his silly behavior than to be likened to him.

GEORGIE PORGIE

Georgie Porgie pudding and pie,

Kissed the girls and made them cry;

When the boys came out to play,

Georgie Porgie ran away.

Head, Shoulders, Knees, and Toes

is the ultimate naming song and you've surely noticed that toddlers love to name things. At first you may worry that your child has OCD (why is he going through his tool kit and announcing its contents again?). But not to worry: naming and cataloging is normal and important. It's the way toddlers learn how the world is organized and the way certain things go with other similar things. The parts of the body are fun to list and the props are always at hand.

Nursery Workout Babies get a kick out of watching this song performed. For maximum effect, do it standing up and every time you say a body part, touch it. (A few rounds at top speed, and you can cut your spinning class and not feel guilty.) Feel free to use other body parts like feet, belly, thighs, and hips; or hair, elbows, heels, and tongue, or any combination that scans (that is, has the same number of syllables or beats).

Head, Shoulders, Knees, and Toes

Head, shoulders, knees, and toes
   (Knees and toes)

Head, shoulders, knees, and toes
   (Knees and toes)

And eyes and ears and mouth and
   nose

Head, shoulders, knees, and toes
   (Knees and toes)

Here We Go Round the Mulberry Bush

is ideal for play in the yard or park. Mulberry trees (they're actually short trees, not bushes) grow throughout England. James I introduced them to the country in the 1600s in the hopes that England could become a major silk producer, mulberry trees being the habitat of the silkworm. Alas, the plan went awry when he planted the wrong variety of mulberry tree.

Déjà Tune "This Is the Way We Wash Our Clothes" (page 156) has the same tune.

HERE WE GO ROUND THE MULBERRY BUSH

Here we go round
   the mulberry bush

The mulberry bush

The mulberry bush

Here we go round
   the mulberry bush

So early in the morning.

Hey Diddle Diddle should be on the cover of a Mother Goose tabloid: "Dish and Spoon Busted in Secret Tryst! Fork Tells All!" It is a towering classic of the nursery canon. The nonsensical zany action and the wonderful alliteration (diddle, fiddle, little) are pleasing to the imagination and the ear. The cow jumping over the moon has become a familiar image, appearing all over the place, and discovered by most kids in the Margaret Wise Brown classic bedtime story *Goodnight Moon*.

Hey Diddle Diddle

Hey diddle diddle

The cat and the fiddle

The cow jumped over
the moon

The little dog laughed

To see such sport

And the dish ran away
with the spoon.

Hickory Dickory Dock

I was astonished to learn that "Hickory Dickory Dock" has only one verse. It seems as if it should have eleven more, each devoted to another number on the face of a clock. Despite its brevity, the nonsense words are peppy and so is the tune.

> Hickory dickory dock
> The mouse ran up the clock
> The clock struck one
> The mouse ran down
> Hickory dickory dock

Wait. . . There's More! Another way to keep "Hickory Dickory Dock" going is to change "dock" to other things. One classic variation is this:

Hickory dickory dare
The pig flew through the air
The man in brown
Soon brought him down
Hickory dickory dare

You can then move on to other nonsense such as:

Hickory dickory dump
The man fell with a bump
He fell from bed and hit his head
Hickory dickory dump

Or

Hickory dickory dive
The bee flew in the hive
We knew because we heard him buzz,
Hickory dickory dive

There is really no limit to where nonsense can take you.

Humpty Dumpty

Humpty Dumpty is an oldie but goodie, another one (like "Frère Jacques") for which variations are found throughout the world. The verse is thought to have originally been a riddle. Why couldn't Humpty be put back together? Because he's an egg. But Lewis Carroll made Humpty so famous in *Through the Looking-Glass* that the riddle no longer works. Some fans of historical interpretation believe that Humpty was a cast-iron cannon that defended the walls of the English city Colchester until it fell down and was smashed to bits; others say he represented Richard III.

Humpty on Toast

"Egg and Soldiers" is a nursery dish beloved by children in England. It is a soft-boiled egg surrounded by toast points. No connection to Humpty has been officially established, but have you ever heard of an egg and soldiers mingling in any other context?

Humpty Dumpty

Humpty Dumpty sat on a wall

Humpty Dumpty had a great fall.

All the King's horses and
  all the King's men

Couldn't put Humpty together
  again.

If All the Raindrops Were Lemon Drops

reminds us of the joy and delight a child takes in things that we take for granted. Like the rain, for instance. For most grown-ups, it's nothing more than a hassle, meaning that we can't wear mascara or suede shoes, and are forced to root around in the closet for an umbrella. For young children, it's a miracle—water is falling from the sky! Snow, with its delicacy, slipperiness, and ability to transform into snowmen and ice forts, is even more wondrous.

Tips for Tots If you're outside, change the words to "I would stand *here* outside . . . ." The "ah-ah-ah-ah" line should be delivered with your tongue sticking out to catch the falling treats.

IF ALL THE RAINDROPS WERE LEMON DROPS

If all the raindrops were lemon drops
    and gumdrops

Oh what a rain that would be!

I would stand outside with my
    mouth open wide

Ah, ah, ah, ah, ah, ah, ah, ah, ah, ah.

If all the raindrops were lemon drops
    and gumdrops

Oh what a rain that would be!

If all the snowflakes were candy bars
    and milk shakes

Oh what a snow that would be!

I would stand outside with my
    mouth open wide

There's more ☞

Ah, ah, ah, ah, ah, ah, ah, ah, ah, ah.

If all the snowflakes were candy bars
and milk shakes

Oh what a snow that would be!

If all the sunbeams were bubblegum
and ice cream

Oh what a sun that would be!

I would stand outside with my
mouth open wide

Ah, ah, ah, ah, ah, ah, ah, ah, ah, ah.

If all the sunbeams were bubblegum
and ice cream

Oh what a sun that would be!

CARPE DIEM

Children make you stop and take a good look at the world around you, helping you realize that even the most ordinary things inspire awe and gladness. The next time it rains, feel the drops plink-plink-plink on your face. Turn your tongue to the sky. Splash in a puddle. Then go inside with your little one, change your clothes, make a cup of cocoa, and watch the raindrops stream on the window pane. Now just imagine if they weren't made of water . . .

MOTHER GOOSE'S ALMANACK

Many verses are dedicated to truisms about weather and seasons and stars and related matters. These rhymes are nice to trot out when the occasion is right, so I urge you to get reacquainted with them.

It's Raining, It's Pouring

It's raining, it's pouring
The old man is snoring
He went to bed and he bumped his head
And he won't get up till morning.

Rain, Rain

Rain, rain, go away.
Come again some other day.

April showers bring May flowers.

Star Light, Star Bright

What could be more fun than wishing on a star?

Star light, star bright,
The first star I see tonight.
I wish I may, I wish I might,
Find the wish I wish tonight.

Travel east, travel west,
After all, home is best.

Red Sky at Night

No doubt about it; sailors know the sky. Next time you see a red sky, check the next day's weather and see if this little poem isn't spot on.

> Red sky at night
> Sailors' delight
> Red sky at morning
> Sailors take warning.

Thirty Days Hath September

This one may feel too old for little ones but it's a classic, it scans well, and it is so incredibly useful, I still recite it to myself when I need to figure out dates. Don't you? Kids may not use it right away but it's well worth having in your repertoire.

> Thirty days hath September
> April, June, and November
> All the rest have thirty-one,
> Except February, which stands alone.

If You're Happy
And You Know It

First you'll do this as a performance piece, but soon, when the baby is one and a half or so, he'll be joining in. This is a great song to help your child develop gross motor skills—large movements like clapping, stomping, raising hands above the head—as opposed to fine motor skills, like picking up a Cheerio with thumb and forefinger.

All Together Now Give two claps after each instance of "clap your hands." You can give either two stomps or—why be stingy?—go crazy and really stomp like you're having a temper tantrum. When you "shout hooray," lift your arms above your head.

There's more ☞

If You're Happy
And You Know It

If you're happy and you know it
    clap your hands

If you're happy and you know it
    clap your hands

If you're happy and you know it
    then you've really got to show it

If you're happy and you know it
    clap your hands.

If you're happy and you know it
    stomp your feet

If you're happy and you know it
    stomp your feet

If you're happy and you know it
    then you've really got to show it

If you're happy and you know it
    stomp your feet,
      clap your hands.

If you're happy and you know it
    shout hooray

If you're happy and you know it
    shout hooray

If you're happy and you know it
    then you've really got to show it

If you're happy and you know it
    shout hooray,
    stomp your feet,
    clap your hands . . . [etc.]

Itsy Bitsy Spider offers fun

for all ages—even the tiniest infants are mesmerized by fingers and hands, and it continues to be of interest to toddlers, who like to mimic the motions with you and, later, sing the words.

This is a spider with an admirable work ethic. He climbs up, he gets rained on, but at his earliest opportunity he climbs right back up again. He is a role model for trying, failing, and trying again. File him away, because there will be times when you can remind your older baby that spiders don't quit and neither should he.

How to Do It

Make the spider climb by placing the thumb of one hand against the forefinger of your opposite hand. Twist your wrist so that the other thumb and forefinger touch. Move your hands upward as you do this. Go, spider, go!

2nd line: Splay all your fingers and wiggle them as you draw your hands downward.

3rd line: Raise your arms straight up and make an arc away from your body.

Last line: Repeat the motions of the first line.

The itsy bitsy
spider went up
the water spout

Down came the rain
and washed the
spider out.

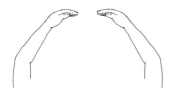

Out came the sun
and dried up
all the rain

And the itsy bitsy
spider went up
the spout again.

Jack and Jill have been the dynamic duo of the nursery for centuries. Extra verses have been added to the rhyme over the years, but they are stilted and out of date. I stick to the classic first verse, but offer the second here in case others like it and are not troubled by Dame Dob's nursing instincts.

Kid Stuff If you are on a gentle, grassy slope and your child is old enough, isn't it the perfect time to take a tumble? Just lie down and roll together.

JACK AND JILL

Jack and Jill went up a hill
To fetch a pail of water
Jack fell down
And broke his crown
And Jill came tumbling after.

Up Jack got and home did trot
As fast as he could caper
To old Dame Dob
Who patched his nob
With vinegar and brown paper.

Jack Be Nimble is a great old chestnut to trot out at that point when your child becomes enthralled with jumping—sometime around age two. Put anything in the middle of the floor (though not a lighted candle, please) to represent the candlestick, and recite the verse as you jump over it. Replace the name Jack with your own child's name if it scans as well.

Don't Try This at Home

If candlestick jumping doesn't seem like a typical activity for children, that's because it wasn't. The activity was an old English form of divination, associated with Saint Catherine, the patron saint of spinsters. On November 25, the saint's feast day, single gals would take turns jumping over a lighted candle. Nobody knows how candlestick jumping made its way into the nursery.

JACK BE NIMBLE

Jack be nimble
Jack be quick
Jack jump over
The candlestick.

Jack Sprat

Dinner at the Sprats' doesn't sound very easygoing, does it? Jack is following a restricted-fat diet, while Mrs. Sprat is apparently on Atkins. But the silver lining is that they complement each other. They are yin and yang, one's excesses filling the other's shortcomings. Put another way: They share and they cooperate.

> Jack Sprat could eat no fat
> His wife could eat no lean
> And so between the two of them
> They licked the platter clean.

Flat Sprat "Jack Sprat" works because it's pleasing to the ear. The flat "a" sounds of the first line are bracing, like a good slap. The rhyme scheme is simple and bouncy. And "licked" is a graphic, fun word.

WHAT'S UP WITH JACK?

He's nimble and quick, but he falls down hills. He likes pie, but he can't abide fat. Who is he? Jack, of course. Jack is one of the great stars of the nursery. He crops up everywhere, getting into all manner of trouble. Why is Jack such a popular guy? I have two theories. First, the sound of the word is strong, masculine, and decisive as well as short and memorable. These are ideal traits for rhyme makers. Second, Jack is short for John, which has been one of the most popular names in the English language for centuries. Jack is a name that many children can relate to and can be viewed as a sort of Everychild name (not unlike our calling an unknown person John Doe).

The name Jack has come back into fashion lately. Its popularity climbs every year, while John's slips. So all of the little Jacks out there have plenty of rhymes just for them.

Lavender's Blue dates from the seventeenth century. It started as a love song, moved to the nursery, then hit the dance floor in the 1940s, and finally returned to the nursery where it has remained. It's a fine pastoral poem, ideal for springtime and summer. Take your toddler to the garden and show him that if he rubs his fingers on the leaves of herbs, he will be able to smell their different fragrances. And if you are eager for more colors and flavors, follow up with the old standard "Roses are red / Violets are blue / Sugar is sweet / And so are you."

LAVENDER'S BLUE

Lavender's blue, dilly, dilly,
Rosemary's green
When I am king, dilly, dilly,
You shall be queen.
Call up your men, dilly, dilly,
Set them to work;
Some to the plow, dilly, dilly,
Some to the cart;
Some to the hay, dilly, dilly,
Some to cut corn;
While you and I, dilly, dilly,
Keep ourselves warm.

Les Petites Marionettes

uses hand motions that are more twisty and flamboyant than most others. The song (on the CD) is about two dancing marionettes, who dance and then hide, dance and then hide. The element of disappearance and reappearance is a thrill for babies.

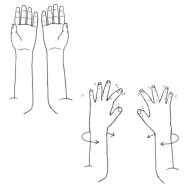

To start, hold your arms in front of you parallel to the floor, your elbows bent at a ninety-degree angle, like TV surgeons before they operate.

Next, twist your hands at the wrist quickly and wiggle your fingers. Keep this up throughout the next two lines.

Then, roll your hands in front of you three times then hide them behind your back ("s'en vont"). Make the dancing motion with your hands again until the last line. Now cradle your arms as though you are rocking a baby to sleep ("dormiront").

Les Petites Marionettes

Ainsi font, font, font
Having fun, fun, fun

Les petites marionettes
They're the dancing marionettes

Ainsi font, font, font
Having fun, fun, fun

Trois petits tours et puis s'en vont.
Three small turns and then they're done.

Mais elles reviendront
Back they run, run, run

Les petites marionettes
They're the dancing marionettes

Mais elles reviendront
Back they run, run, run

Quand les enfants dormiront.
At the setting of the sun.

Little Bo Peep

Most people know that little Bo Peep is the careless shepherdess who mislaid her flock, but few can recite beyond the first two lines. Here is the whole shebang.

> Little Bo Peep has lost her sheep,
> And can't tell where to find them;
> Leave them alone and they'll come home,
> Wagging their tails behind them.
>
> Little Bo Peep fell fast asleep,
> And dreamt she heard them bleating;
> But when she awoke, she found it a joke,
> For they were still all fleeting.

Then up she took her little crook,
Determined now to find them;
She found them indeed, but it made
    her heart bleed,
For they'd left their tails behind them.

It happened one day, as Bo Peep did stray
Into a meadow hard by,
There she espied their tails side by side,
All hung on a tree to dry.

She heaved a sigh, and wiped her eye,
And over the hillocks went rambling,
And tried what she could,
    as a shepherdess should,
To attach each again to its lambkin.

Little Boy Blue is about a shepherd who slacks off at work. Some scholars say the poem is a criticism of Cardinal Wolsey (known as the "boy bachelor" and a confidant of Henry VIII), who was vilified by the public for enriching his own coffers from the wool trade at their expense. Others take it at face value, seeing it simply as a pleasant, pastoral verse that depicts images you might find in the countryside during summer and fall.

LITTLE BOY BLUE

Little Boy Blue,
Come blow your horn,
The sheep's in the meadow,
The cow's in the corn;
But where is the boy
Who looks after the sheep?
He's under a haystack,
Fast asleep.
Will you wake him?
No, not I,
For if I do,
He's sure to cry.

Little Jack Horner's

appeal is not obvious. A child sitting alone in a corner eating a whole pie with his hands? Sounds like an antisocial glutton. But children like the idea of eating with their hands, and like to figure out how to do things themselves and are liberal with self-praise when they succeed. So they relate to little Jack. You can mime the action of sticking out your thumb and scooping up a plum if you like.

Little Jack Horner

Little Jack Horner sat in a corner,
Eating his Christmas pie.
He stuck in his thumb,
    and pulled out a plum,
And said, "What a good boy am I!"

Little Miss Muffet

Miss Muffet isn't the only one who gets scared at this verse. Many parents are put off by all the unfamiliar words. Fear not: A tuffet is a patch of grass (think *tuft*). Curds and whey are basically the solids and liquid, respectively, found in cottage cheese. This poem is a good tickling opportunity. Your hand can become a spider running toward your own Miss Muffet. Just wait until she's finished eating her curds and whey before you tickle.

> Little Miss Muffet
> Sat on a tuffet
> Eating her curds and whey;
> Along came a spider
> Who sat down beside her
> And frightened Miss Muffet away.

TICKLED PINK

What is the most important part of the body where tickling is concerned? The fingers? The back of the knee? The neck? The armpits? None of these. It's the brain. Although our skin is very sensitive, what's most important for effective tickling is suspense. Studies of tickling have revealed both that we can't tickle ourselves (we can predict our own moves) and that the knowledge that a tickle is imminent is enough to make us squirm and giggle. So the next time you prepare to tickle, realize that the thrill lies as much in the anticipation as in the touch.

Tickling can be done with fingers, hair, or with your lips. You'll quickly learn from your baby what she likes. Kiss-tickles on bare skin, blowing, or making nibbling movements with your lips are all fun, but observe your baby for any sign that she's not enjoying it. A vigorous tickling session is definitely not advised right before bedtime because it gets kids all revved up.

London Bridge

is traditionally sung while two children hold hands facing one another and other children go under the bridge formed by their arms. The bridge falls down at the discretion of the two children creating it, trapping one of their friends. Note that the song which dates to the 1600s builds with each verse (the increasing improvement in building materials is reminiscent of the story of the three little pigs).

LONDON BRIDGE

London Bridge is falling down,
Falling down, falling down.
London Bridge is falling down,
My fair lady.

Build it up with rocks and clay,
Rocks and clay, rocks and clay.
Build it up with rocks and clay,
My fair lady.

Rocks and clay will wash away,
Wash away, wash away.
Rocks and clay will wash away,
My fair lady.

There's more ☞

Build it up with iron and steel,
Iron and steel, iron and steel.
Build it up with iron and steel,
My fair lady.

Iron and steel will bend and bow,
Bend and bow, bend and bow,
Iron and steel will bend and bow,
My fair lady.

Build it up with silver and gold,
Silver and gold, silver and gold,
Build it up with silver and gold,
My fair lady.

Silver and gold will be stolen away,
Stolen away, stolen away.
Silver and gold will be stolen away,
My fair lady.

Hire a man to watch
  all night,
Watch all night, watch
  all night.
Hire a man to watch all night,
My fair lady.

London Bridge is falling down,
Falling down, falling down.
London Bridge is falling down,
My fair lady.

Lullaby and Good Night by Brahms is one of the best of the genre. Everything about it is soothing: the tempo (triple meter, slow and rhythmic like the beat of a mother's heart). The key of B-flat is simple and soothing, and the words are repetitive and comforting. Baby is sleeping on Mother's (or Dad's) breast under a canopy of stars. All is right with the world.

Lullaby And Good Night

Lullaby and good night,
In the sky stars are bright,
Close your eyes, start to yawn
Pleasant dreams until dawn.
Close your eyes now and rest
Lay your head on my breast.
Go to sleep now and rest
May your slumber be blessed.

KIDDIE LIT

Poetry has thrived throughout the course of civilization and most of it has been for grown-ups. There are plenty of verses for adults, however, that are also pleasing to children. You probably had to memorize a few lines in high school or college, and they may leap to mind at some point: On many a trip to the mall Wordsworth's immortal "The world is too much with us; late and soon, / Getting and spending, we lay waste our powers" has leapt to my mind. And Shakespeare's Henry V's battle call "Once more unto the breach, dear friends" occurs to me at the threshold of crowded kiddie parties. Why not share your love of literature and the fruits of your fancy college degree with your child? Here are a few of my favorites to get you started.

"She Walks in Beauty" by George Gordon, Lord Byron (in praise of dark-haired girls)

"Pied Beauty" by Gerard Manley Hopkins (a celebration of nature, the seasons, and imperfection)

"The Tyger" ("Tyger, tyger, burning bright") by William Blake
(tigers—*roar!*—in a pleasing rhyme scheme)

"Sonnet 18" ("Shall I compare thee to a summer's day?")
by William Shakespeare (easy and breezier than most
sonnets by the bard)

"On First Looking into Chapman's Homer" by John Keats
(how some experiences in life are so awe-inspiring they
change you forever)

"The Passionate Shepherd to His Love" by Christopher Marlowe
(bouncy rhyme of shepherd wooing a nymph)

"The Nymph's Reply to the Shepherd" by Sir Walter Raleigh
(the nymph's saucy—and vocabulary-rich—reply)

"Lines Written in Early Spring" by William Wordsworth
(pastoral verse at its best)

"I like to see it lap the miles" or "It's all I have to bring today"
by Emily Dickinson (simplicity to be enjoyed on many levels)

"The Road Not Taken" by Robert Frost
(pensive American masterpiece about choice)

Mary Had a Little Lamb

was the first verse, actually the first few *words*, ever recorded. Thomas Edison spoke them into his new recording machine in 1877 and to his delight was able to play them back. It's fitting Edison chose the verse, which is one of the few nursery classics that is American. The poem was written by Sarah Hale and published in Boston in 1830. Others later tried to claim the verses as their own, most notably Mary Tyler, who lived in Sudbury, Massachusetts. A little red schoolhouse in Sudbury is still celebrated as related to the rhyme.

Sing It To convert the poem to a song, just add a little echo:

Mary had a little lamb,
Little lamb, little lamb,
Mary had a little lamb,
Its fleece was white as snow;
And everywhere that Mary went
Mary went, Mary went,
And everywhere that Mary went,
The lamb was sure to go . . .

Mary Had a Little Lamb

Mary had a little lamb,
Its fleece was white as snow;
And everywhere that Mary went
The lamb was sure to go.

It followed her to school one day,
Which was against the rule;
It made the children laugh and play
To see a lamb at school.

And so the teacher turned it out,
But still it lingered near,
And waited patiently about
Till Mary did appear.

Why does the lamb love Mary so?
The eager children cry;
Why, Mary loves the lamb, you know,
The teacher did reply.

Mary, Mary, Quite Contrary

Mary, Mary, Quite Contrary, also known as "Mistress Mary, Quite Contrary," is one nursery rhyme about whose hidden meaning folks love to speculate. Is "Mary" Bloody Mary, the Catholic monarch who wished to restore her religion to the land by any means necessary? Silver bells could be church bells or instruments of torture. Pretty maids could be nuns, or the guillotine. Makes for a dramatic picture, but there is no evidence that this rhyme relates to the queen at all.

MARY, MARY, QUITE CONTRARY

Mary, Mary, quite contrary,

How does your garden grow?

With silver bells and cockle shells,

And pretty maids all in a row.

Hop, Skip, Jump The rhyme scheme of this verse makes it a good one to chant while jumping rope.

Oh Mr. Sun may seem saccharine to you, but your little one will love it. I like its whiff of pagan ritual—the sun is treated almost as a deity (with the honorific Mr.) and the children are praying to him for favors. Very ancient Egypt.

Finger Play On the first line, put your hands in an arc above your head to represent the sun. For the "Peekaboo" line, put your hands in front of your face ("hiding behind a tree"), then pop your face out. For the last stanza, repeat the arc of the sun. Then wiggle your fingers downward to represent the rays of the sun shining down on you.

OH MR. SUN

Oh Mr. Sun, Sun, Mr. Golden Sun,
Please shine down on me.
Oh Mr. Sun, Sun, Mr. Golden Sun,

Hiding behind a tree. (Peekaboo!)
These little children are asking you,
To please come out so we can play with you,

Oh Mr. Sun, Sun, Mr. Golden Sun,
Please shine down on
Please shine down on
Please shine down on me.

Old King Cole

Old King Cole may have been from Colchester in England or a Welshman named Coel or a tradesman named Colebrook. His pipe may be a wind instrument and the bowl a drum. His rhyme has been around since at least the sixteenth century, and you can see why. It's a jolly little number.

Air Violin Pretend to play the fiddle during the "twee tweedle dee" bit. And feel free to dance around.

OLD KING COLE

Old King Cole
Was a merry old soul
And a merry old soul was he;
He called for his pipe,
He called for his bowl,
And he called for his fiddlers three.

Now every fiddler, he had a fiddle,
And a very fine fiddle had he;
Twee tweedle dee, tweedle dee,
   went the fiddlers.
Oh, there's none so rare
As can compare
With King Cole and his fiddlers three.

Old MacDonald is great for long car rides, trips to the petting zoo, and anytime you just feel like making animal noises. Among the first sounds kids love to imitate are animal sounds. You can sing the song in the straightforward way, or you can make each verse build by tacking on the previous animal sounds to each new one. It's a fun little memory game that works like "Alouette" (page 20).

MacDonald Mix-'N-Match

Here are some other suggestions for animals and their sounds. The possibilities are nearly endless.

- chicken (bok-bok)
- pig (oink-oink)
- mouse (squeak-squeak)
- horse (neigh-neigh)
- owl (hoo-hoo)
- cat (meow-meow)
- goat (meh-meh)
- sheep (baa-baa)
- dog (woof-woof)
- turkey (gobble-gobble)
- snake (sss-sss)
- crow (caw-caw)
- lion (roar-roar)

Old MacDonald

Old MacDonald had a farm
     E-I-E-I-O
And on that farm he had a cow
     E-I-E-I-O
With a moo-moo here and a moo-moo there,
Here a moo, there a moo,
Everywhere a moo-moo.
Old MacDonald had a farm
     E-I-E-I-O

Old MacDonald had a farm
     E-I-E-I-O
And on that farm he had a duck
     E-I-E-I-O
With a quack-quack here and a quack-quack there,
Here a quack, there a quack,
Everywhere a quack-quack.
Old MacDonald had a farm
     E-I-E-I-O

Old Mother Hubbard always

struck me as the ultimate lousy housekeeper. Then I had a baby and suddenly I totally understood her plight. (Hey, it's tough to keep the pantry stocked when you have a busy life.) When I learned the whole rhyme—not just the slightly downbeat first verse—my feelings for her changed again. Mother Hubbard may not be perfect, but she loves her little pup so much that she will go to any length to please him, no matter how outrageously he behaves. Now she's my hero.

The simple rhyme scheme of this poem is pleasing to little ears. It's the kind of repetitive verse that might put a baby to sleep if you simply read it. But it can be jazzed up for toddlers if you act out some of the words, like laughing when the dog does, miming playing a flute and putting on a coat and wig, offering a "meee" for the goat, and dancing a jig.

Old Mother Hubbard
Went to the cupboard
To fetch her poor dog a bone;
But when she got there
The cupboard was bare
And so the poor dog had none.

She went to the baker's
To buy him some bread;

There's more ☞

But when she came back
The poor dog was dead.

She went to the undertaker's
To buy him a coffin;
But when she came back
The poor dog was laughing.

She went to the tavern
For white wine and red;
But when she came back
The dog stood on his head.

She went to the market
To buy him some fruit;
But when she came back
He was playing the flute.

She went to the tailor's
To buy him a coat;
But when she came back
He was riding a goat.

She went to the barber's
To buy him a wig;
But when she came back
He was dancing a jig.

The dame made a curtsy,
The dog made a bow;
The dame said, "Your servant,"
The dog said, "Bow-wow."

One, Two, Buckle My Shoe is an agreeable way to help start your child counting. The progression in the poem suggests that a parent and child are going outside—getting dressed, closing the door, and running to the henhouse. "One, Two, Buckle My Shoe" dates to at least the late eighteenth century and appears in variations throughout the world. Versions of the verse count up to thirty, but the words are dated and the rhymes lame past ten. "Seventeen, eighteen / Maids in waiting"? No, thanks. I stop before the poem jumps the shark.

Let Your Fingers Do the Talking With each number, hold up the correct amount of fingers, and mime the actions as you recite them. You can wag your finger for "Don't be late" and give a big "bok, bok, bok" at the end.

ONE, TWO, BUCKLE MY SHOE

One, two,
Buckle my shoe.
Three, four,
Shut the door.
Five, six,
Pick up sticks.
Seven, eight,
Don't be late.
Nine, ten,
A big, fat hen.

Open, Shut Them

This song introduces the very basic concept of open versus closed. Notice that your hands are the star of the verse, but they are never actually named.

Open, shut them
> *Open your hands and splay your fingers wide
> then snap hands closed*

Open, shut them
> *Repeat*

Give a little clap, clap, clap.
> *Clap three times*

Open, shut them

Open, shut them

Lay them in your lap, lap lap.
> *Pat your lap three times and rest your hands there*

Creep them, crawl them,
> *Walk your fingers up toward your face*

Creep them, crawl them,

Right up to your chin, chin, chin.

Open wide your little mouth

But do not let them in.

Wiggle your fingers in front of your closed mouth

HAND JIVE

Hands are a source of endless fascination to babies. They seem to have lives of their own and they have nearly acrobatic abilities. They can represent spiders, squid, rain, and sun. They can make an entire person disappear—or so it seems in a good game of peekaboo. They can dance (see "Les Petites Marionettes," page 72), they can issue instructions (What does the policeman say with his hand up? "Stop!"), they can tickle, they can count, and they can soothe. They are always, ahem, on hand. So if you have left the house without a toy or a snack or you find yourself facing a long wait in a doctor's examination room, no need to panic. Remember that you have all the entertainment and comfort you need right at your own fingertips.

Patty Cake must be the ultimate nursery verse. It offers comfort in a soothing, regular meter, in the repetition of the first phrase, in the subject matter (cake, yum!), and in the image of a parent and baby sharing a cozy, nurturing activity together.

If you scratch the surface, the imagery and words of "Patty Cake" suggest the creation of a baby itself: Babies are often thought of as buns in the oven, and pregnancy is long and slow, and most women wish it could be over faster.

Patty Cake Primer Clap your hands throughout the first two lines. If you want to be fancy about it, you can clap as though you are patting a little piece of empanada dough: patting down one way and then twisting your wrists to pat facing the other way. Roll your hands around each other and then fold them as though you were folding the sleeves of a T-shirt. Trace the shape of a *B* on the baby's tummy or in the palm of her hand. At "put it in the oven," slide one hand straight out as though you are putting a cookie sheet in the oven, then bring the other down onto it, so your palms are closed together.

PATTY CAKE

Patty cake, patty cake,
  baker's man,

Bake me a cake as fast
  as you can

We roll it and fold it and
  sign it with a B,

And put it in the oven
  for baby and me.

OVERHEARD AT THE PLAYGROUND

‑ ‑

Here is a miscellany of traditional playground chatter, including, in ascending order of complexity, a cheer, a jeer, a retort, an adjudicator, and a fact.

I Scream, You Scream

When it's summer and you are standing in the playground as the ice-cream truck approaches, this is what to shout.

> ✓ I scream, you scream,
> We all scream for ice cream!

I See London

Careful with this one. If you say it with a mischievous smile on your face when you see a diaper peeking out of a onesie, and if you tickle a chubby thigh at the same time, it's all in good fun. If you do it with a *nyah-nyah* tone of voice, then you risk hurting feelings.

> I see London, I see France
> I see someone's underpants!

What to Say to the Bully Who Calls You Names

Sticks and stones may break my bones,
But names will never hurt me.

One Potato

The potato game is used to determine who will be "it" or go first. Everybody stands in a circle and holds out two fists. These are the potatoes. The person counting takes his closed fist and counts off the other potatoes, using his own chin as his second potato.

One potato, two potato, three potato, four,
five potato, six potato, seven potato, more.

The potato first hit on "more" is "out." The last potato left in the circle is "it."

Goodbye, Columbus

Columbus sailed the ocean blue
In fourteen hundred ninety-two.

Pease Porridge Hot

was a street hawker's cry in the Middle Ages. Pease porridge was the medieval equivalent of split pea soup, and it was often served on Sundays during Lent. How it became a traditional children's song is anybody's guess. Perhaps some poor sleep-deprived mother of yore was just desperate enough to turn a commercial slogan into a diversion for her babe. Who could blame her?

Easy Peasy Porridge

Here's my recipe for quick and tasty pease porridge.

> 3 tablespoons olive oil or butter
> 1 onion, peeled and chopped
> 6 cups chicken or vegetable stock
> 2 cups split peas (or red lentils)
> 1 potato, peeled and chopped
> Salt and pepper to taste
> Freshly chopped parsley to taste

In a soup pot, heat the oil over medium heat. Add the onion and sauté until soft and lightly golden, about five minutes. Add the stock, peas, and potato, and cook over medium-high heat until boiling. Turn down the heat to a simmer, cover, and cook for an hour. Check as it cooks and add water if it becomes too thick. Stir in salt, pepper, and a sprinkle of parsley, and serve with crusty bread.

Pease Porridge Hot

Pease porridge hot!
Pease porridge cold!
Pease porridge in a pot,
Nine days old.

Some like it hot,
Some like it cold,
Some like it in the pot
Nine days old.

Peter Piper existed before the turn of the nineteenth century, but in 1813 he became the star of a booklet published in England called *Peter Piper's Practical Principles of Plain and Perfect Pronunciation.* The text offered tongue twisters for every letter of the alphabet; they were used to amuse and to help speakers with their elocution. Perhaps because he was the headliner, "Peter Piper" is the guy we still recite today.

Math for Moms A peck is equivalent to about 2 gallons. So Peter Piper picked an awful lot of pickled peppers.

PETER PIPER

Peter Piper picked a peck
    of pickled peppers
A peck of pickled peppers
    Peter Piper picked.
If Peter Piper picked a peck
    of pickled peppers,
How many pickled peppers
    did Peter Piper pick?

Pío, Pío, Pío is a nursery classic in the Spanish-speaking world. It's a sweet little song on the surface with a lovely melody, but it's actually rather dramatic. Baby chicks are hungry, cold, and crying; the hens must find them food and comfort and nestle them for warmth. This is life-and-death stuff. The drama is underscored by the structure of the verse, which essentially boasts a narrator and a chorus, and thus reminds me of an opera. Interwoven in the narrator's story is the plaintive chorus of the chicks' "pío, pío, pío."

Pío, Pío, Pío

Los pollitos dicen "pío, pío, pío"
The baby chicks say "pío, pío, pío"
Cuando tienen hambre
Whenever they are hungry
Cuando tienen frio
Whenever they are chilly.

Las gallinas buscan el maiz y el trigo
Then hens look for corn and wheat
Para los pollitos "pío, pío, pío."
For the baby chicks "pío, pío, pío."

Le dan la comida
They give them food
Y pone abrigo
And keep them warm
Para los pollitos "pío, pío, pío."
For the baby chicks "pío, pío, pío."

THERE'S NO BUSINESS
LIKE SHOW BUSINESS

Children of all ages love theatricality. Don't feel that you have to sing nursery rhymes in a pretty way for your child. Ham it up. Experiment.

For example, sometimes I keep "Pío, Pío, Pío" light and airy and sing it straight. Other times, I do the opera version, slowing it down so it's like a melancholy aria sung with deep feeling. I become the mother hen narrator, cold, hungry, living on a winter farm with not enough grain to go around, in charge of a desperate brood. I turn toward the limelight and sing . . . .

At the first "pío, pío, pío" I move my hands as though I have chick puppets on them and as though the chicks are singing the words. At "Cuando tienen hambre" I rub my tummy. At "Cuando tienen frio" I wrap my arms around myself and shiver in the lonely, frigid barnyard. At "Las gallinas buscan" I scan the ground looking in vain for corn and wheat. Ideally, at the next "pío, pío, pío" I have someone else—my skeptical, reluctant husband, usually—pipe up as the chorus. I put my hand to my ear as I listen to the chorus of chicks singing.

At "Le dan la comida" I mime giving food to the chicks. At "Y pone abrigo" I cross my arms across my chest and rub, as I think about warming up. And again, I listen to the sad cry of the barnyard and sing along on the last "pío, pío, pío." I perform encores upon request.

Try taking other classic nursery songs and translate them into other styles. Here are some of my favorite ways of doing so that have met with great success from my peanut gallery:

"Oh Mr. Sun": this is essentially a plea, not unlike the song "Sandy" from *Grease*

"Do Your Ears Hang Low?": My friend Margaret's husband sings the song once through, then Margaret answers him in her best basset hound voice

"Head, Shoulders, Knees, and Toes": Pretend you are Ethel Merman and sing this one. It's never been better, right?

"Skip to My Loo": Time to trot out the southern accent

"The Noble Duke of York": I often sing it like Rex Harrison, complete with British accent

Pop Goes the Weasel started

life hundreds of years ago as a tavern song and somehow migrated to the children's playroom. To kids, it's a lively song featuring animals chasing one another, shiny pennies, and a recipe for a sweet rice pudding. Not to mention the *Pop!* line, which has a hide-and-seek appeal.

To curious grown-ups there is more going on: The song is all about money and the want of it. To "pop" means to pawn something. And a weasel could refer to a winter coat (in cockney rhyming slang, *weasel and stoat* means "coat") or to the shuttle used by weavers, which could also have been pawned in lean times. The third verse is about a humble pudding. The fourth describes a pub crawl—the Eagle was a London tavern. What is the singer pleading about in the fifth verse? Either he wants to stay out late with the lads at the Eagle and/or he needs a few more bob for the next round.

Pop Goes The Weasel

Round and round the cobbler's bench
The monkey chased the weasel,
The monkey thought 'twas all in fun
Pop! Goes the weasel.

A penny for a spool of thread
A penny for a needle
That's the way the money goes
Pop! Goes the weasel.

A half a pound of tuppenny rice
A half a pound of treacle
Mix it up and make it nice
Pop! Goes the weasel.

There's more ☞

Up and down the London road
In and out of the Eagle
That's the way the money goes
Pop! Goes the weasel.

I've no time to plead and pine
I've no time to wheedle
Kiss me quick and then I'm gone
Pop! Goes the weasel.

TWO LINES AND TO BED

Sleep, and my son's desire to avoid it at all costs, has been a major issue in our home. We've read all the books, tried all the tricks, and finally, nearly three years into his life, things are better. We have a couple of bedtime routines that work well, all of which involve reading several books and ending on ones that are signals to sleep, including the classic *Goodnight Moon* by Margaret Wise Brown and contemporary bestseller *Pajama Time!* by Sandra Boynton. Sometimes there is a lullaby worked in—"Fais Dodo" (page 36) or "Lullaby and Good Night" (page 86) are favorites. No matter what routine we use we always end on the same note, with this two-line classic that serves as a punctuation mark. It says to my son in utterly clear terms: "That's it. Party's over. See you in the morning." At a glance, it seems like a dreary little couplet. Why bring up the subject of insect infestation right before bed? But it actually adds a nice dash of levity to a bedtime routine that used to be fraught with stress and tremendous effort.

Good night, sleep tight,
And don't let the bedbugs bite.

Pussycat, Pussycat, Where Have You Been?

must be recited with a healthy dose of affectation to pull off properly so that the word "been" rhymes with "queen."

Charming anecdotes exist about queens Victoria and Elizabeth II each being asked by children about her pussycat or mouse. The queen here, however, is believed to be the first Queen Elizabeth. The rhyme has contemporary resonance for many readers of Ludwig Bemelmans's Madeline series: In *Madeline in London,* when the girls return home, the housekeeper asks where they've been, and the girls quote the second line of this verse.

Pussycat, Pussycat, Where Have You Been?

Pussycat, pussycat,
    where have you been?

I've been to London
    to see the queen.

Pussycat, pussycat,
    what'd you do there?

I frightened a little mouse
    under her chair.

Ring Around the Rosie is

one of the great classics of nursery verse with dark associations. Many people believe it dates back to the days of the Black Plague, which ravaged London in the seventeenth century: The plague creates a rosy complexion; flowers were carried in handkerchiefs in the belief that their pleasing smells could ward off the disease; ashes and falling down relate to death. Folklore experts Iona and Peter Opie aren't convinced. They point out that gifted children were thought to "laugh roses" and that the falling down action was a curtsy in some older versions.

Ring Leader Everybody holds hands and moves in a circle for the first two lines. Then everybody drops to the floor. For the second verse, pound hands on the floor for "thunder." Make craggy, pointing motions for the lightning with your hands. Bring hands in an arc above your head to simulate sun.

RING AROUND THE ROSIE

Ring around the rosie
A pocketful of posies
Ashes, ashes, we all fall down.

An Optional Coda

The sheep were in the meadow
Huddled all about
There was thunder
And lightning
And then the sun came out.

Rock-a-Bye Baby baffles parents. What's up with the baby falling out of a tree? The song is the best-known lullaby in the English language and has been around since at least the eighteenth century. The rhythm of the music is certainly soothing—a triple meter that is reminiscent of a human heartbeat and common to lullabies. Maybe the baby is really falling into sleep or into the safety and comfort of a parent's arms.

ROCK-A-BYE BABY

Rock-a-bye baby,
   on the treetop

When the wind blows
   the cradle will rock

When the bow breaks
   the cradle will fall

And down will come baby,
   cradle and all.

Row, Row, Row Your Boat is about time.

Having a baby creates a whole new sense of clock and calendar. On the one hand, life speeds up and there's a desperate scramble to keep balls in the air—to make dinner, soothe tears, squeeze in some work. To paraphrase Jane Austen, it whizzes by in a swirl of busy nothings. But within that crazy whirlwind are pockets of stillness. One morning you may awaken at six and find that you have a whole day stretching in front of you. Maybe you and your toddler will take two hours to walk a few blocks to the post office to mail a letter, counting pebbles along the way, running a stick along the fence in front of the library, and singing. Or maybe you awaken from a nap and roll over to gaze at the face of your newborn, still sleeping. You never tire of just looking at her sweet face, those pouty lips, that button nose. And as you gaze it feels like time stretches into eternity. "Row, Row, Row

Your Boat" brings that back to me. Motherhood is a river. Sometimes there are waves and strong tides and it takes my full attention to stay afloat. Other days, all is calm, and I can just drift, letting the sun envelop me and time melt into the shore.

Row, row, row your boat
Gently down the stream,
Merrily, merrily, merrily, merrily,
Life is but a dream.

Sassy Variation for Older Tots

Row, row, row your boat
Gently down the stream,
If you see an alligator,
Don't forget to scream.

Rub-a-Dub-Dub

This verse reminds me of the Rat Pack: rub-a-dub-dub makes me think of ring-a-ding-ding. So snap your fingers, plop your kid in the tub, and scrub away.

> Rub-a-dub-dub
>
> Three men in a tub
>
> And who do you think they be?
>
> The butcher, the baker,
>   the candlestick maker,
>
> Turn 'em out—knaves, all three!

Shoo Fly

This American folk song has a tempo that suggests a country dance and is ideal for skipping. Have the kids wave their hands around their heads to "shoo" the fly away. It ends on a lovely warm note; it's nice to feel you belong to someone.

Shoo, fly! Don't bother me.
Shoo, fly! Don't bother me.
Shoo, fly! Don't bother me.
I belong to somebody.

I feel, I feel, I feel like a morning star.
I feel, I feel, I feel like a morning star.

Shoo, fly! Don't bother me.
Shoo, fly! Don't bother me.
Shoo, fly! Don't bother me.
I belong to somebody.

Sing a Song of Sixpence

is a wonderful, ridiculous song. During medieval times pies filled with live birds were served at banquets. The pie was cut open and guests were very surprised when the birds escaped and flew around the room.

Because of its fanciful imagery and the age of the verse (it dates to the sixteenth century), diverse speculations about its origins abound. One of the most colorful is that it was a covert advertisement for pirates to work with the notorious Blackbeard. Legend says that sixpence and a ration of rye was the salary being offered and that blackbirds are Blackbeard's pirates who would spring on unsuspecting ships. The king is Blackbeard himself, leader of the pirates, and the dainty dish set before him is the booty.

SING A SONG OF SIXPENCE

Sing a song of sixpence,
A pocket full of rye;
Four and twenty blackbirds
Baked in a pie.
When the pie was opened,
The birds began to sing;
Now wasn't that a dainty dish
To set before the king?

There's more ☞

The king was in his counting house,
Counting out his money;
The queen was in the parlor
Eating bread and honey.
The maid was in the garden
Hanging out the clothes,
When along came a blackbird
And snipped off her nose.

There Goes Your Nose At the end of the verse, play
"I've Got Your Nose." Make a fist and use your knuckles to
"pinch" off the child's nose. After you pinch, stick your thumb
(the child's nose) through your folded fingers and wiggle it.

LIE BACK AND THINK
OF ENGLAND

Many nursery classics are *veddy, veddy* British, having been passed down through generations and across the seas. Several boast pastoral imagery—"As I Was Going to St. Ives," "Little Boy Blue," and "Mary, Mary, Quite Contrary" leap to mind. Others feature traditional British foods—Christmas pie ("Little Jack Horner"), treacle ("Pop Goes the Weasel"), and tarts ("The Queen of Hearts"). Not to mention all the distinguished personages: queens, kings, knaves, dukes, ladies, masters, parsons, and more. Anglophile moms and dads will not be disappointed by the color and atmosphere of the nursery canon.

Skip to My Loo

appeals to the youngest kids because they can babble "loo, loo, loo." Older kids love it because it's perfect for skipping and square dancing.

"Skip to My Loo" adapts incredibly well to variations. Lots of extra verses abound, many of them from the square dancing circuit, where this song is well loved with lines like "Off to Texas, two by two." The "oo" sound works really well with children's interests. Make up your own custom verses. Try "Cows in the cornfield. Moo, cow, moo." Or "Ghosts in the attic. Boo, ghost, boo." Or "I lost my sandal, where's that shoe?" Or "Nice to meet you. How do you do?" The possibilities are endless.

Skip To My Loo

Loo, loo, skip to my loo,
Loo, loo, skip to my loo,
Loo, loo, skip to my loo,
Skip to my loo my darling.

Fly's in the buttermilk. Shoo, fly, shoo!
Fly's in the buttermilk. Shoo, fly, shoo!
Fly's in the buttermilk. Shoo, fly, shoo!
Skip to my loo, my darling.

Loo, loo, skip to my loo,
Loo, loo, skip to my loo,
Loo, loo, skip to my loo,
Skip to my loo, my darling.

There's more ☞

I lost my partner, what shall I do?
I lost my partner, what shall I do?
I lost my partner, what shall I do?
Skip to my loo, my darling.

I'll find another one, prettier'n you,
I'll find another one, prettier'n you,
I'll find another one, prettier'n you,
Skip to my loo, my darling.

Loo, loo, skip to my loo,
Loo, loo, skip to my loo,
Loo, loo, skip to my loo,
Skip to my loo, my darling.

SQUARE DANCE 101

"Skip to My Loo" almost begs to be sung while square dancing. Here are a few of the basic moves to learn and teach to a toddler.

Forward and Back: Dancers are facing one another. One at a time, they take three steps toward their partner, point a foot, then take three steps back.

Dos-si-dos: Facing one another, dancers advance toward one another, then pass each other, brushing right shoulders. After they've passed, they walk backward past one another, brushing left shoulders.

Swing: Dancers hold hands and twirl in a circle. (See if you can get some lift with a toddler—they love that.)

Arm Turns: Dancers link arms and twirl around one another.

Promenade: Dancers link arms and march around the room (in a pinwheel shape if there are multiple couples).

Clapping: When your hands are free, clap to the beat.

Slowly, Slowly Creeps the Garden Snail

is a nice one for babies who love to have the palms of their hands tickled. Keep it in your repertoire for times when you've forgotten to bring a toy and the baby is getting restless or when you can't get to a toy immediately—like in the car. You can tell an older child the joke about the snail and his car: Snail goes into a car dealership and buys the fastest car they have. He asks to have an S painted on the side. Why? So when people see him pass they'll say "Look at that S-car go!" (Get it? Escargot. S-car go.)

SLOWLY, SLOWLY CREEPS THE GARDEN SNAIL

Slowly, slowly creeps
the garden snail

Creep your index finger slowly around baby's palm

Slowly, slowly up
the wooden rail

Run it up baby's middle finger

Quickly, quickly runs
the little mouse

Use all fingers to make the mouse run all over the palm . . .

Quickly, quickly round
about the house.

. . . and then run over and around the entire hand

Teddy Bear, Teddy Bear

can be recast so the part of the teddy bear is played by any other three-syllable character you like—pussycats, honeybees, elephants, puppy dog, etc. I often do; I just don't think it's fair that Teddy Bear always gets star billing. And besides, teddy bears don't make the fun noises that other animals do. If you are working with another animal you can meow, buzz, trumpet, or woof after the verse is over.

The Action The motions are easy—just follow the words and twirl, touch, show, etc.

Teddy Bear, Teddy Bear

Teddy Bear, Teddy Bear, twirl around.
Teddy Bear, Teddy Bear, touch the ground.
Teddy Bear, Teddy Bear, show your shoe.
Teddy Bear, Teddy Bear, that will do.

Teddy Bear, Teddy Bear, climb the stairs.
Teddy Bear, Teddy Bear, say your prayers.
Teddy Bear, Teddy Bear, turn off the light.
Teddy Bear, Teddy Bear, say good night.

The Green Grass Grows All Around

Here's a kids' song you can really sink your teeth into, exercising your memory while you're at it.

> There was a hole
> In the middle of the ground
> The prettiest hole
> That you ever did see
> And the green grass grows all around and around
> And the green grass grows all around.
>
> There was a tree
> In the middle of the hole
> The prettiest tree
> That you ever did see
> Well, the tree in the hole
> And the hole in the ground

And the green grass grows all around and around
And the green grass grows all around.

And on that tree
There was a branch
The prettiest branch
That you ever did see
Well, the branch on the tree
And the tree in the hole
And the hole in the ground
And the green grass grows all around and around
And the green grass grows all around.

And on that branch
There was a nest . . . [etc.]

And in that nest
There was an egg . . . [etc.]

And in that egg
There was a bird . . . [etc.]

The Noble Duke of York

can be great fun for baby and a fabulous workout for Mom. Feel those abs engage as the baby trots up and down the hill that you create with your knees. You will get the biggest up-and-down effect if you're on the floor with your legs stretched out as you perform this. It can also be done while seated in a chair, but the differences between high and low are more subtle. In my experience, the duke rarely takes just one trip. Prepare yourself for several sallies up the hill.

THE NOBLE DUKE OF YORK

The Noble Duke of York
Trot for first two lines

He had two thousand men

He marched them up to the top of the hill
Knees way up

And he marched them down again
Knees down

And when they're up, they're up
Shoot knees up

And when they're down, they're down
Take knees down in one motion

And when they're only halfway up
Knees halfway up

They're neither up nor down.
(Shoot up)   *(Shoot down)*

The Queen of Hearts

The Queen of Hearts that sticks in most of our minds is the impatient sovereign of Lewis Carroll's Wonderland who terrorized poor Alice, shouting, "Off with her head!" The queen of this nursery rhyme, who is almost a hundred years older than Carroll's monarch, is a much more domestic creature. Her rhyme is sweet and summery, and justice prevails in the end.

> The Queen of Hearts she baked some tarts
> All on a summer's day.
> The Jack of Hearts, he stole those tarts
> And hid them all away.
>
> The King of Hearts heard of those tarts
> And to the Jack did say,
> "You Jack of Hearts, return our tarts
> Or else for them, you'll pay!"

The Wheels on the Bus

I had never heard "The Wheels on the Bus" before I had a child. Now I can't imagine my life without it. It's not a traditional song dating back hundreds of years (how could it be?), but it's a contemporary classic that belongs in every new parent's repertoire. Preschoolers are fascinated by wheels and vehicles of all kinds, especially big ones. And the only thing better than riding a bus is pretending you *are* a bus (and later in the verse, a passenger).

There's more ☞

THE WHEELS ON THE BUS

The wheels on the bus go round and round
Round and round, round and round
The wheels on the bus go round and round
All through the town.

The doors on the bus, they open and shut
Open and shut, open and shut
The doors on the bus, they open and shut
All through the town.

The windows on the bus go up and down
Up and down, up and down
The windows on the bus go up and down
All through the town.

Additional Verses

The wipers on the bus go swish, swish, swish…
The driver on the bus says, "Move on back!"…
The baby on the bus says, "Waaa! Waaa! Waaa!"…
The mommy on the bus says, "Sssh! Sssh! Sssh!"…
The daddy on the bus says, "I love you!"…

Who's On the Bus? You can play fast and loose with these lyrics. We've added coins that go "clink, clink, clink" and then updated the bus fare to a card that goes "swipe, swipe, swipe." And I've been on buses that have essentially stopped to pick up all of Old MacDonald's farm—there have been chickens bok-bok-boking, and cows moo-moo-mooing, and so on. You never know who's going to board a bus these days.

This Is the Church, This Is the Steeple

This Is the Church, This Is the Steeple is a traditional finger play that dates to the nineteenth century. Here is how you can play: Fold your hands together with your fingers on the inside, next to your palms. For the steeple, raise your two index fingers to meet. For "Open it up" turn your hands over and open them, keeping your fingers crossed—your fingers are the congregants. For the alternate lines, close your hands around the churchgoers. Then, one by one, straighten each finger up—that's the parson going upstairs. For the last line, your palms are facing in prayer.

THIS IS THE CHURCH, THIS IS THE STEEPLE

This is the church

This is the steeple

Open it up

And see all the people.

Alternate Last Lines

Here is the parson,
    going upstairs

Here is the parson,
    saying his prayers.

This Is the Way We Wash Our Clothes

Ah, domestic bliss! Everything is in order: the washing, the cleaning, the baking is done—and it's not even lunchtime. For many of us, this song does not reflect the realities of our households, so it may need a few tweaks. "Sweep the floor" sometimes becomes "Vacuum dirt." And "morning" is more likely to be "evening" at my house. But no matter, babies love the simple mimed hand movements, and toddlers delight in helping with chores. They like to feel useful working alongside Mom or Dad. I've been told to enjoy it while it lasts.

> This is the way we wash our clothes,
> Wash our clothes, wash our clothes,
> This is the way we wash our clothes,
> So early in the morning.

This is the way we iron our clothes,
Iron our clothes, iron our clothes,
This is the way we iron our clothes,
So early in the morning.

This is the way we fold our clothes,
Fold our clothes, fold our clothes,
This is the way we fold our clothes,
So early in the morning.

This the way we sweep the floor,
Sweep the floor, sweep the floor,
This is the way we sweep the floor,
So early in the morning.

This Little Piggie is a classic

ryhming game for anyone enthralled by toes—and really, who isn't? Kids love being tickled on their feet and they love to look at other people's toes and feet as well. Feet are usually hidden so it's fun when they come out to play. And toes seem to have a life of their own, which is fun and surprising.

Vary the words as much as you like. I was thirty-two years old and astonished to learn that most piggies go to market rather than to Boston, which was where they went in the version recited in my Massachusetts home.

Vegetarian Version If you don't eat meat, your piggies shouldn't either. Feel free to substitute another two-syllable foodstuff for the roast beef. I know piggies who dine on tofu, spinach, and yogurt, as well as treats like French toast, sorbet, and cupcakes. In fact, if you wanted the piggies to eat really well-balanced meals you could challenge yourself to find a new food for them every time you recite this.

This Little Piggie

This little piggie went to market,

Wiggle baby's big toe between your thumb and index finger

This little piggie stayed home,

Wiggle second toe

This little piggie ate roast beef,

Wiggle middle toe

This little piggie had none,

Wiggle fourth toe

And this little piggie cried, "wee, wee, wee" all the way home.

Wiggle the little toe and then run your fingers up the baby's foot and leg as far as you can get

This Old Man is the tune that the children's television show *Barney* so successfully adapted into a number called "I Love You." The original version is more whimsical, less saccharine, and a fine way to start learning how to count.

Additional Verses

The verses continue in a very predictable pattern. Feel free to swap the words for others that rhyme.

Three: knee
Four: door
Five: hive
Six: sticks
Seven: up in heaven
Eight: gate
Nine: spine
Ten: pen

THIS OLD MAN

This old man, he played one
He played knick-knack on my thumb
With a knick-knack, paddy whack
Give a dog a bone
This old man came rolling home.

This old man, he played two
He played knick-knack on my shoe
With a knick-knack, paddy whack
Give a dog a bone
This old man came rolling home.

Three Blind Mice

An early version of "Three Blind Mice" was published in 1609 in a book of rounds. The lyrics have mutated over the years but the blind mice and the violence have remained. Nobody knows why a song involving blindness and butchery caught on in the nursery. Maybe because the tune is so irresistible.

Three blind mice,
Three blind mice,
See how they run,
See how they run,
They all ran after the farmer's wife,
Who cut off their tails with a carving
knife.
Did you ever see such a sight in your life
As three blind mice?

CHILDPROOF WORLD

One of my worries before I had a child was that I was going to enter a world where no more sharp edges existed. The pointy coffee table and the sarcasm would both have to go. I would be surrounded by things that are soft and fuzzy and sweet and cute all the time.

Things are softer and sweeter now, but I have realized that childhood is not without a fascination for things that are dangerous. Many classic nursery rhymes are filled with upsetting doings: The Three Blind Mice are assaulted; the children of "The Old Woman Who Lived in a Shoe" don't have enough to eat and are beaten; etc. With fairy tales it only gets scarier; kids will encounter orphans and wolves and getting lost and so on.

Should you shy away from violent rhymes or expose your child to them? I have gone back and forth on the question and now go with my gut. I like "Three Blind Mice" and my son seems untroubled by it, so we sing it. I think the shoe-dwelling family is too sad, so I skip that one. My feeling is that life is filled with adversity and in manageable doses a bit of it is good for children. It teaches them self-reliance and empathy and caution and reminds them they are lucky as well as resilient.

Three Little Kittens is like

a big bowl of oatmeal: good for you, yet warm and comforting at the same time. It teaches us about responsibility and cause and effect. By the end of the verse the kittens understand that if they aren't careful with their things, they won't get a reward. All the imagery is warm and fuzzy (kittens and mittens and pie, oh my!).

THREE LITTLE KITTENS

Three little kittens, they lost their mittens
So they began to cry,
Oh mother dear, we sadly fear that we have lost
  our mittens.
What? Lost your mittens, you naughty kittens!
Then you shall have no pie.
Meow, meow, meow.
No, you shall have no pie.

Three little kittens, they found their mittens
And they began to cry,
Oh mother dear, see here, see here, for we
  have found our mittens.
Put on your mittens, you silly kittens,
And you shall have some pie.
Meow, meow, meow.
Oh, let us have some pie!

There's more ☞

The three little kittens put on their mittens,
And then ate up the pie.
Oh mother dear, we greatly fear that we have
  soiled our mittens.
What? Soiled your mittens, you naughty kittens!
Then they began to sigh.
Meow, meow, meow.
Then they began to sigh.

The three little kittens they washed their mittens,
And hung them out to dry.
Oh mother dear, do you not hear
That we have washed our mittens?
What? Washed your mittens, then you're good
  kittens,
But I smell a rat close by.
Meow, meow, meow.
We smell a rat close by.

THE CRADLE WILL ROCK

This book is all about celebrating tradition. Tradition is great, of course. Classic nursery verses bind us to our forebears, giving childhood a common bond, and ensure that what you sing to your child is effective, having been tested for eons. But sometimes you want to break out of the box. Tired of the same old thing, you want to shake things up. When that happens to me I turn to the songs of my adolescence in the 1980s. You might be surprised at how effectively pop songs can be converted to the nursery. Sometimes you have to tweak a word here or there, or slow down a crazy punk beat, but that's easy to do. Here are some of my own Top Forty picks:

Sell Me a Coat by David Bowie (chilly, Dickensian imagery—great for winter)

Planet Earth by Duran Duran (or *Rio* or *Save a Prayer* or almost anything else…)

I Wanna Be Sedated by the Ramones (slow it down and it's perfect for bedtime)

La Isla Bonita by Madonna (innocuous lyrics but not too treacly, like *True Love*)

Livin' on a Prayer by Bon Jovi (worth it for the chorus)

Rock Lobster by the B-52's (makes SpongeBob seem totally normal)

Dancing with Myself by Billy Idol (obviously you have to dance while you sing)

Karma Chameleon by Culture Club (vintage Boy George, before the fall)

To Market, to Market to Buy a Fat Pig

may be one you're already familiar with. It's short and catchy, making it easy to remember. It contains fun, broad words, both nonsense (jiggety-jig and -jog) and real (fat, pig, hog). Kids love pigs, and if the pig is fat, well, that's even better.

TO MARKET, TO MARKET
TO BUY A FAT PIG

To market, to market, to buy a fat pig,
Put your child on your lap and trot your legs to the left

Home again, home again, jiggety-jig.
Trot back to the right

To market, to market, to buy a fat hog,
Trot to the left and oink after the line if you like

Home again, home again, jiggety-jog.
Trot to the right

Here's a traditional variation
for kiddies who don't eat pork

To market, to market, to buy a plum bun,
Home again, home again, market is done.

Trot, Trot to Boston is the

way I learned this delightful game, probably because Boston was my hometown and Lynn a nearby suburb. But if for some reason you don't want your baby trotting around random New England cities, you can replace "Boston" with any two-syllable place. Then replace "Lynn" with "town" and "in" with "down."

Before the Fall "Trot, Trot to Boston" is the kiddie equivalent of a roller-coaster ride—it's all about anticipating that fall and the thrill of surviving it.

Trot, Trot To Boston

Trot, trot to Boston
Put your child on your lap and bounce up and down

Trot, trot to Lynn
Keep bouncing

Careful when you get there
Still bouncing

You don't fall in!
Spread your legs apart and let the child "fall"
(careful, please) almost to the floor

TROTTING ALONG, SINGING A SONG

Babies love the sensation of trotting and bouncing and bumping along on your lap. They look as exhilarated as if they were riding on a real camel or horse or buggy. The thrill of possible danger—*I might fall!*—makes it even more exciting, without being too scary—*But Mom is holding me tightly.* Vary your trotting styles for interest. "Alice the Camel" might trot with just a raise and lower of your feet on the floor. The horse that rides to Boston might trot with alternating raises and lowerings of your feet (lots of uneven cobblestones in a colonial city). And when you are riding in the Noble Duke of York's brigade, things can be really bumpy—*I make his men move very quickly.*

Twinkle, Twinkle, Little Star

is one of the few enduring nursery rhymes whose author is known. Jane and Ann Taylor, English sisters, published a book of children's poetry in 1806. One of Jane's contributions was called "The Star," which we've come to know as "Twinkle, Twinkle, Little Star." The music that we associate with the verse is believed to have been taken from a French song from the late eighteenth century.

Star Satires

Many parodies of the poem exist. The best of the bunch is from *Alice's Adventures in Wonderland* when the Mad Hatter must sing a silly variation for the Queen of Hearts. His riff went like this:

Twinkle, twinkle little bat!
How I wonder what you're at!
Up above the world you fly,
Like a tea-tray in the sky.
Twinkle, twinkle little bat!
How I wonder what you're at!

There's more ☞

Twinkle, Twinkle, Little Star

Twinkle, twinkle, little star,
How I wonder what you are!
Up above the world so high,
Like a diamond in the sky.

When the blazing sky is gone,
When he nothing shines upon,
Then you show your little light,
Twinkle, twinkle, all the night.

Then the traveler in the dark,
Thanks you for your tiny spark,
He could not see where to go,
If you did not twinkle so.

In the dark blue sky you keep,
And often through my curtains peep,
For you never shut your eye,
Till the sun is in the sky.

As your bright and tiny spark,
Lights the traveler in the dark,
Though I know not what you are,
Twinkle, twinkle, little star.

Wee Willie Winkie is the Scottish version of the Sandman. He's the sprite who brings sleep to us and leaves crumbly "sand" that we find in our eyes upon waking. Somehow the sandman never really hit it big in traditional verse, but Wee Willie Winkie did. WWW is like a town crier crossed with a sandman. He runs around town visiting homes and making sure that all the kids are tucked in for the night. The poem in which he stars was written by William Miller in 1841. I've translated it here from the original Scots.

WEE WILLIE WINKIE

Wee Willie Winkie runs through the town,
Upstairs and downstairs in his nightgown,
Rapping at the window, crying through the lock,
"Are the children in their beds? For now it's
    eight o'clock."

Hey Willie Winkie, are you coming in?
The cat is singing lullabies to the sleeping hen,
The dog is lying on the floor and doesn't hear
    a peep,
But here's a wakeful child, who will not fall
    asleep!

There's more ☞

Anything but sleep, the imp! He's glowing like the
   moon,
Rattling like an iron jug with an iron spoon,
Rumbling, tumbling round about, crowing like a
   cock,
Shrieking like I know not what, waking sleeping folk.

Hey, Willie Winkie, the child's taken heel,
Wiggling off his mother's knee like a slippery eel,
Tugging at the cat's ear, mocking all her moans,
Hey, Willie Winkie, look out, here he comes!

Weary is the mother who has a restless babe,
A chubby little bunny, who longs to run all day,
Who has a battle every night; he'll not go gently he,
But one kiss from his rosy lips gives newfound
   strength to me.

THERE'S NO VERSE LIKE OM

We have all experienced the total munchkin meltdown. The next time your infant (nine months or younger) is inconsolable and it's not an issue of feeding or changing, and you've rocked and you've sung until you can rock and sing no more, try the yoga *OM*. Press the baby to your chest, take in a deep breath, and chant "*Ommmmm*" in her ear, holding the note as long as you can.

OM is Hinduism's elemental mantra and is thought to represent the sound the universe made at its creation. There is mounting evidence that vibrations of the kind generated by the sound *om* have healing properties. The sound has been found to lower blood pressure, slow and regulate breathing, relax muscles, and quiet the mind.

Try it during the next crying jag and if it doesn't turn the baby from crabby to contemplative, it might at least give you a little stress relief.

Where Is Thumbkin?, sung to

the tune of "Frère Jacques," is essentially a polite conversation between the fingers of the left hand and those of the right. It's also a chance to name your fingers and try to articulate each of them separately—fine motor skills that, as you shall discover, are particularly challenging for middle and ring fingers.

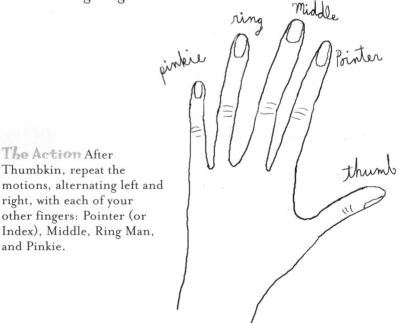

The Action After Thumbkin, repeat the motions, alternating left and right, with each of your other fingers: Pointer (or Index), Middle, Ring Man, and Pinkie.

WHERE IS THUMBKIN?

Where is thumbkin?

Where is thumbkin?

Wiggle your left thumb

Here I am. Here I am.

Wiggle your right thumb

How are you today sir?

Wiggle your left thumb

Very well, I thank you.

Wiggle your right thumb

Run away. Run away.

Put both hands behind your back

THESE ARE THE RHYMES
THAT TRY MOMS' SOULS

Not every nursery rhyme deserves equal consideration. Just because it's old or because others like it doesn't mean you have to. Here are a handful I dislike and would never recite to my child or any other. I include them here, at the back, with my thoughts on why not to use them, because even if you don't like something, it's better to be informed than ignorant. Besides, you may disagree with me and be able to put them to good use.

Peter, Peter, Pumpkin Eater

There's plenty of violence in children's verses (page 163) and some of it, I can bear. But Peter putting his wife in a pumpkin shell? It's too much for me. The rhyme is so famous you're probably familiar with it, but it's not one I like to use.

Peter, Peter, Pumpkin Eater
Had a wife and couldn't keep her,
Put her in a pumpkin shell,
And there he kept her very well.

There Was a Little Girl
Who Had a Little Curl

My mother used to recite this to my sister who had curly hair—but only when she was misbehaving. Guess how that made her feel? She still cringes at the sound of it.

There was a little girl
Who had a little curl
Right in the middle of her forehead.
When she was good she was very, very good
And when she was bad she was horrid.

Monday's Child

My child was not born on a Wednesday, but what if he had been? Although I wish I had a good rhyme for learning the days of the week, I don't use this one in solidarity with all the little Wednesday kids (and Thursdays and Saturdays too) who've been unfairly labeled.

Monday's child is fair of face,
Tuesday's child is full of grace,
Wednesday's child is full of woe,
Thursday's child has far to go,
Friday's child is loving and giving,
Saturday's child works hard for a living,
But the child that's born on the Sabbath day
Is bonny and blithe and good and gay.

The Old Woman Who Lived in a Shoe

If you want to feel really good about your parenting, remind your kids about the old woman who lived in a shoe. They could have it much worse.

There was an old woman
    who lived in a shoe,
She had so many children
    she didn't know what to do.
She gave them some broth
    without any bread,
Then spanked them all soundly
    and put them to bed.

CD Recording: The Songs

1. ABC Margaret, Rebecca & Carolyn **2. Alice the Camel** Carolyn, Rebecca & Margaret **3. Alouette** Carolyn **4. A Tisket, A Tasket** Margaret, Rebecca & Carolyn **5. Baa, Baa, Black Sheep** Rebecca & Margaret **6. Clean Up, Clean Up** Rebecca, Carolyn & Margaret **7. Do Your Ears Hang Low?** Rebecca & kids **8. Down by the Station** Rebecca, Carolyn & Margaret **9. Fais Dodo** Margaret & Carolyn **10. Frère Jacques** Margaret, Rebecca & Carolyn **11. Head, Shoulders, Knees, and Toes** Ensemble & kids **12. If All the Raindrops Were Lemon Drops . . .** Ensemble & kids **13. If You're Happy and You Know It** Ensemble & kids **14. Itsy Bitsy Spider** Rebecca, Margaret & Carolyn **15. Les Petites Marionettes** Jennifer Griffin **16. London Bridge** Carolyn, Margaret & kids **17. Lullaby and Good Night** Margaret **18. Mary Had a Little Lamb** Jamie **19. Oh Mr. Sun** Rebecca **20. Old MacDonald** Carolyn, Rebecca & Margaret **21. Open, Shut Them** Rebecca **22. Pío, Pío, Pío** Carolyn **23. Pop Goes the Weasel** Rebecca **24. Rock-a-Bye Baby** Rebecca **25. Row, Row, Row Your Boat** Carolyn, Rebecca & Margaret **26. Shoo Fly** Margaret, Rebecca & Carolyn **27. Sing a Song of Sixpence** Carolyn, Rebecca & Margaret **28. Skip to My Loo** Rebecca, Margaret & Carolyn **29. The Green Grass Grows All Around** Rebecca & kids **30. The Noble Duke of York** Carolyn & kids **31. The Wheels on the Bus** Carolyn, Rebecca & kids **32. This Is the Way We Wash Our Clothes** Margaret **33. This Old Man** Carolyn **34. Three Blind Mice** Jamie **35. Twinkle, Twinkle, Little Star** Rebecca & Margaret

Performed by singers Rebecca Kendall, Carolyn Montgomery, Margaret Murphy, and Jennifer Griffin plus The Good Mood Singers (kids): Helen Handelman, Nancy Handelman, Jacob Lawrence Kreiss, Carmen Lawrence, Nicole Melkonian, Lena Schwartz. Instruments: *Guitars, Ukulele, Harmonica,* Vinnie Zummo; *Bass, Tuba,* Dave Hofstra; *Percussion,* Rex Benincasa; *Piano, Harmonium, Percussion, Melodica, Synthesizers,* Jamie Lawrence.